I0450171

Whales

For Kids

Amazing Animal Books for Young Readers

John Davidson
Mendon Cottage Books

JD-Biz Publishing

All Rights Reserved.
No part of this publication may be reproduced in any form or by any means, including scanning, photocopying, or otherwise without prior written permission from JD-Biz Corp and http://AmazingAnimalBooks.com. Copyright © 2015

All Images Licensed by Fotolia and 123RF

Read More Amazing Animal Books

Table of Contents

10 Wonderful Facts about Whales

Blue whale is known to be the largest mammal that has ever lived, having a length of up to 105ft and weighing nearly 150 tons, the same weight as 150 small cars.

Whales being mammals have to come up for air unlike fish which can breathe under water.

Whales do not sleep very long because they have to remember to come up for air.

Whales breathe in air through their blowhole.

The female Baleen whale is larger than the males.

Male whales are referred to as the bulls, females as the cows and their young ones as calves.

The Beluga whales are very sociable and vocal and they can even make facial expressions.

The brain of the whale only sleeps one half at a time, this is because the other half needs to make sure the basic functions such as breathing go on.

Baleen whales, which are Humpback, Right, Blue and Fin whales, have no teeth.

The Humpback whale can eat up to a ton of food each day.

Types of Whales

Whales are largest aquatic mammals. They breathe through lungs unlike other animals which breathe through gills. Whales have streamlined bodies. This enables them to move or swim freely through water .in fact, they are the only mammals known to live in water as well as adapted to stay in the open oceans.

There are various types of whales. They can be categorized into groups basing on the features they have. That is, their sizes, shapes, predators, where they live and many more other factors.

Blue whale is one of the most famous types of the mammals. It is the largest of all and also the loudest animals on earth. They can weigh up to two hundred tons. They also live in cold conditions.

We also have orca, which are the most powerful predators. They are known to hunt together in pods of forty .There average life span in between seventy to ninety years.

What do whales eat?

Whales are very big animals. They need to eat a lot of food to live. Whales eat more food than other animals. Whales are divided into two kinds.

There is the tooted and the baleen whale. They both eat different kinds of food. Toothed whales have large teeth. They eat fish, squids and seals. Some whales eat dolphins. Others eat each other.

Whales can group together and eat larger animals than themselves. This is because it will make it easier to kill a larger animal when they are large numbers.

The Baleen whales does not have large teeth like the toothed whale. They have structures called baleen. This helps them to filter the food that they eat.

Food is trapped by these baleen structures on the whale. This makes it easy for the whale to feed on the trapped food. The baleen whales eat smaller food like plankton, small fish and krill.

Where do Whales Live

Whales are one of the largest mammals in most continents. They are warm blooded animals. There are different types of whales in this world.

They live in various places in the world. Some inhabit along major oceans in the world. That is, from arctic oceans or Antarctic oceans to tropical waters. On the other hand, they can also live around the canter of the equator.

There are reasons as to why whales do not live at same places. One of them is migration. They move from one place to another in such of food. During this period, they tend to drift apart, so that they can be able to satisfy their needs.

While some species, especially those with big sizes may not live same ground with those with small sizes. Those with large bodies can survive in cold places, while those with small bodies may not. This gives us a reason as to why they may live in different places.

How Do Whales Communicate?

Whales are one of the largest mammals we have in the world. Just like all other mammals, whales can breathe, they can nurse their young ones through breast feeding.

Besides; whales are also warm blooded animals. They also have a skin blubber made up of fats to store some energy, hence acting as an insulator.

There exists an advanced form of exchange of words among these mammals. This is what we call communication.

This is when they make use of sound waves in echolocation so as to detect organism as well as objects by sonar. Then the sound which they produce, bounces off the object in water, hence returning the whale in the form of an echo.

Echoes are very essential in helping the mammals get a judgment of the shape, size, speed as well as the size.

Finally, it is a bit interesting with sonar waves, in that they can travel more than a kilometre per second. Some whales like Baleen are known to generate loudest sounds on earth.

How big are Whales?

Whale sizes vary greatly is size as per the species. The largest species of whale is the blue whale. They are able to grow to an average length of between 70 to 80 feet, however, in some occasions, the blue whales measures over 100 feet in length and the largest blue whale often weighs over 150 tones.

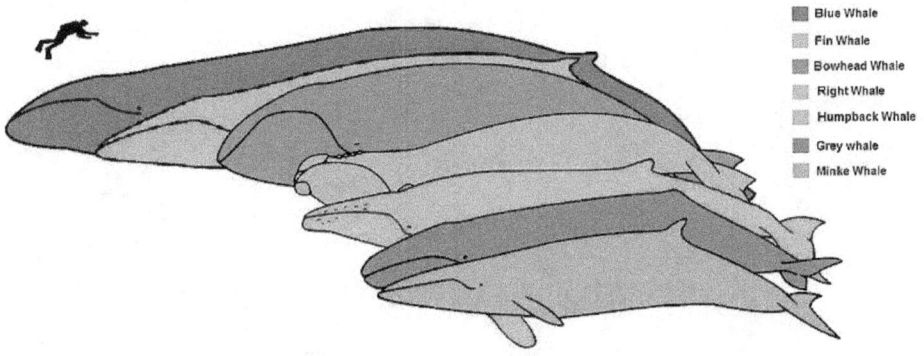

Size chart from Wikimedia Commons

The heart of a blue whale can weigh over 1,300 pounds. The dwarf sperm is the smallest species of whale and it weighs roughly 600 pounds and measures only 9 feet.

As a matter of fact, the dwarf whale is very small that it can take up around 11 dwarf sperm whales which are lined up in a row for them to measure up to a 100 feet blue whale.

Right whale can measure an average length of up to 60 feet with an average weight of up to 60 tons.

The gray whale species can measure an average length of 45 to 48 feet and has an average weight of up to 40 tons.

Do whales sleep?

You may be asking yourself, do whales sleep? The answer is yes- whales do sleep, but in a unique manner different from other sea creatures and mammals.

Unlike fish which use gills to breathe; whales, which are mammals, use blowholes found on top of their heads to take in air, a process that requires them to come to the water surface constantly.

To avoid suffocation and drowning, a whale will always breathe in a huge amount of air to last it sometime underwater.

As they are voluntary breathers, whales will breathe only when it's necessary. To sleep without risk of drowning, a whale will rest one half of its brain. This lets the whale sleep in a semi-conscious state, while at the same time reducing oxygen usage.

As such, the mammal will be able sleep for some time before having to go for air, letting it get some rest. This state of semi-sleep is similar to napping in humans.

Baby Whales

In case a female whale becomes pregnant, it carries her baby inside her up to for 17 months; this is the same as 1 year and 5 months. This period where the female whale carry's the baby inside her is known as the gestation period.

After 17 months are over the female whale is ready to give birth. The baby whale (calf) will come out with its head or its tail first. The baby whale's birth takes place in the water.

The female whale can give birth to a baby whale at anytime of the year. When it is born, the baby whale can weigh from 300-400 pounds and it can be up to 8ft long.

The baby whale can nurse for almost 12 months. The baby whale drinks up to 500 litres of its mother's nutritious milk every day.

The baby whales stick close to their mother till they are old enough to live and eat by themselves.

Whale Migration

The migration habits of whales are quite fascinating and are interesting to observe. Whales mostly migrate from north to south especially along the American coast during different seasons.

During the migration, the whales head out in search of food rich areas which they visit yearly. In the process, they take advantage of the warmer waters along the equator during winter and head out to the cooler waters closer to the poles during summer.

Humpback whale family or pod.

The arctic region is usually food-rich during the warmer months which play out well killing two birds with one stone. The migration to warmer waters also acts as an opportunity for the mother whales to give birth to young calves.

The migration is usually very long with some such as the Grey whales which are believed to travel the furthest, covering up to 10,000 miles which is overwhelming. The range of travel is wide meaning it is quite hard to tell the migration routes especially in the deep seas.

Types of whales

Whales are largest aquatic mammals. They breathe through lungs unlike other animals which breathe through gills.

Whales have streamlined bodies. This enables them to move or swim freely through water in fact, they are the only mammals known to live in water as well as adapted to stay in the open oceans.
There are various types of whales. They can be categorized into groups basing on the features they have. That is, their sizes, shapes, predators, where they live and many more other factors.

Blue whale is one of the most famous types of the mammals. It is the largest of all and also the loudest animals on earth. They can weigh up to two hundred tons. They also live in cold conditions.

We also have orca, which are the most powerful predators. They are known to hunt together in pods of forty .There average life span in between seventy to ninety years.

Baleen whales

The Baleen whales are one of the largest whales in the world. They are also known as whalebone whales and also as great whales. These whales are characterized by their baleen plates for the filtration of food from water in spite of teeth.

Baleen whales

The Blue Whale, the largest animal known is also included in the group of these whales. These whales have 2 blowholes which causes a V-shaped blow. These whales are generally found in small groups known as pods. Despite of their tremendous size, they are able to leap out of water. They can grow to about 190,000 kilograms in weight and in about 33 m (108 ft) in length.

Beluga whales

Beluga whales are mostly found in temperate waters of Scandinavia and Greece .During winter they usually migrate to the coast of Patagonia. They can grow up to an average length of 32 feet.

Beluga whales

Beluga's body's weight can reach 7 tons. Beluga whales can live as long as seventy five to one hundred years. The major foods consist of harp seal and tuna as they are carnivorous. It is rare for Beluga whales to attack a human being. They give birth to their young ones called Piddlins, usually they give birth to babies which can be 7 or 8 in total.

Their total population on earth is approximated to be over

17million. While females are social living in fronds, male Beluga whales are known to be solitary.

Blue Whales

Blue whales are the largest animals in the world. They are from the Baleen species of whales. Blue whales can grow up to unbelievable sizes of about 100ft in length and weigh nearly 160 tons. They have a mottled bluish gray colour, their heads are flat and broad, and they have a dorsal fin.

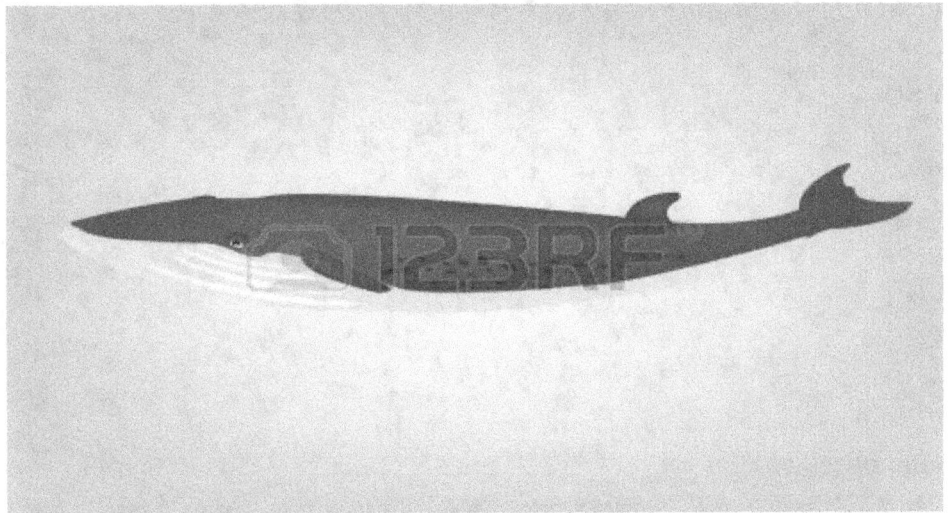

Blue Whale

The heart of the blue whale is the size of a small car and it pumps up to 10 tons of blood throughout the enormous body of the whale.

Blue whales can be found in all of the world's oceans. They can occasionally be seen swimming in groups but most of the time they swim alone or in pairs. Most Blue whales practice seasonal migration based on weather conditions.

Grey whales

Grey whales are mostly found in shallow waters in the Eastern North Pacific Ocean. Humpback is one of the gray whales. Humpback whales are about 50 feet long and weigh approximately 48 tons each. They have large flippers which makes them distinct from the rest of the whales.

Humpback whales

They have different colours ranging from black to grey but have markings that are white in their undersides .The markings are distinct for each humpback whale and can be used by scientists for identifying individual whales just like finger prints in man.

They like shallow waters and live in large groups of up to

20,000 whales. Male humpback whales produce songs when mating which is a distinct characteristic in them. They majorly rely on krill and fish for food.

Killer whales

The Killer whales are one of the most dangerous whales in the world. These whales are part of the oceanic dolphin family and are toothed whales. They are also called Orca whales and sometimes also known as blackfish. The killer whales are found in all the oceans, from Arctic Ocean to the Antarctic Ocean.

Killer whale

They are highly social as they live in a group. Each group has about 40 whales. Some killer whales feed on fish and some

hunt other marine mammals such as seals, sea lions, walruses and even other whales. They are regarded as apex predators as there are no predators above them in the food chain.

The Resident killer whales, the Transient killer whales and the offshore killer whales are the three types of the Killer whales. They are long distant travellers and are found in colder coastal water but the killer whale pods are seen all around the world from the Equator to the Poles.

Killer whales

Several Interesting Facts about Orca Whales

One species of sea mammals that always captures the attention of so many people are the Orca whales. These creatures are quite amazing animals and are the largest sea mammals in the dolphin family. Here are some other interesting facts about these beautiful and powerful creatures. The name, Orca is Latin and means the Greek God of the Underworld. The size of this type of whale is huge, as an Orca whale is around 20 to 26 feet in length and its body weight is about 6 tons and Their colour is black and white.

Three Orca killer whales

The Orca whales live mostly in tropical climates as well as the Arctic waters. They are social animals and like to live among a group of whales and they hunt, share food and protect their young as well as other whales that are vulnerable.

The Orca whales communicate and hunt with the use of

echolocation, which is a way to produce sound that will help to reveal an objects shape, size and location. The diet for the Orca whale consist of seals, fish, walruses, sea lions, turtles, penguins, sharks, seagulls and even other whales.

Sperm whales

Sperm whales which are also known as "cachalot" are a type of the extended whale family. They have been named like so because of a waxy substance semi-liquid in nature, found in their large heads called spermaceti. They are the largest toothed whales with a male adult measuring up to twenty feet in length and 57,000 kilogram's body in weight.

Sperm whale

Their heads represent almost one third of their entire body and it houses the biggest brain of all animals on earth. They feed on sea creatures called squids. When hunting, the sperm whales can dive for three kilometers, hence the deepest diving mammals. They communicate to each other through clicking sounds with a loudness of 230 decibels underwater, this is also the loudest sound that can be produced by any living creature. They live across the ocean in groups called pods which are made up of the mothers and their calves.

Whales and Dolphins:

The Unique and Interesting Mammals of the Sea
The Ocean is full of marine life and two sea animals that get plenty of attention are whales and dolphins. Two interesting things about these types of sea creatures are that they are not only beautiful but highly intelligent as well.

Marine biologist spend many hours researching the behavior and habits of whales and dolphins, as they are truly an interesting and unique mammals of the ocean.
There are several facts about whales and dolphins that many people find to be quite interesting.

These types of sea animals have a very unique way of investigating their surroundings through the use of echolocation, which creates sounds to their brains.

In regards to the way they eat, they do not chew any food, but instead they swallow their food whole. The fin on the backs of whales and dolphins are called the dorsal fin.

Whales and dolphins are known as cetaceans, as they are sea creatures without hind limbs and use a blowhole for their ability to breathe. Their diet consists of fish, crabs, shrimp and octopus.

Endangered Whales

The following are endangered whales due to different reasons
1. Bowhead whales. They are threatened by the ever increasing melting sea and offshore drilling which destroy their habitats.

2. Gray whales. Their population has been greatly reduced by commercial whaling which threatens their existence.

3. Humpback whales .The major threat of their existence is the commercial whaling

4. Right whales. They were highly hunted by man in the 18th century .People believed they were right whales to hunt as they were readily found at the shores where they can be reached easily. They were also able to float on water after being killed which made it easier for hunters to collect them.

5. Sei whales. They were threatened due to hunting activities

6. Toothed whales. They were endangered due to hunting.

7. Belugas. They were threatened by subsistence hunting

8. Narwhales. They have been hunted by subsistence hunters and industrial whalers

Our books are available at

1. Amazon.com

2. Barnes and Noble

3. Itunes

4. Kobo

5. Smashwords

6. Google Play Books

Publisher

JD-Biz Corp

P O Box 374

Mendon, Utah 84325

http://www.jd-biz.com/

Mendon Cottage Books

P O Box 374, Mendon Utah 84325

Top Ten Dog Breeds For Kids

Amazing Animal Books
For Young Readers

Kisha Bennett & John Davidson

Poodles

Dog Books for Kids

K. Bennett

Labrador Retrievers

Dog Books for Kids

K. Bennett

German Shepherds

Dog Books for Kids

K. Bennett

Rottweilers

Dog Books for Kids

K. Bennett

Boxers

Dog Books for Kids

K. Bennett

Golden Retrievers

Dog Books for Kids

K. Bennett

Beagles

Dog Books for Kids

K. Bennett

Yorkies

Dog Books for Kids

K. Bennett

www.ingramcontent.com/pod-product-compliance
Lightning Source LLC
Chambersburg PA
CBHW061945280526
45787CB00004B/1730